Liberating the Future from the Past?
Liberating the Past from the Future?

by

Erika Schelby

Liberating the Future from the Past?
Liberating the Past from the Future?

Copyright © 2013 by Erika Schelby

ISBN: 978-0-9891216-2-0
Published by Lava Gate Press

Design Selection: Erika Schelby. Layout: Brian Lorelle.
Image Attribution: created by Wolfgang Beyer with the
program Ultra Fractal 3. File: Mandel zoom 00, mandelbrot
set JPG from Wikimedia Commons, License Share Alike 3.0
http://creativecommons.org/licenses/by-sa/3.0/

Interior layout by BookNook.biz.

For Frederick

Author's Note

When the Berlin-based cultural magazine LETTRE INTERNATIONAL organized its philosophical essay competition, it received 2,481 submissions in seven languages from 123 countries. Juries chose 33 authors as finalists: the following essay is one of these short-listed papers.

The contest was held in cooperation with WEIMAR 1999 – selected as European City of Culture – and the Goethe Institute. Weimar is a small place with a big artistic and intellectual heritage. Today it has about 65.000 inhabitants. The term Weimar Republic (1919-1933) is probably better known than the town itself – Germany's first democratic constitution was signed here. In the late 18th and the first decades of the 19th century the city was the center of literary classicism, with famed writers like Goethe and Schiller in residence. Carl Philipp Emanuel Bach was born there, and Walter Gropius founded the Bauhaus School in Weimar. Wassily Kandinsky, Paul Klee, Oscar Schlemmer, and Lyonel Feininger were among its teachers.

Media coverage about the essay contest was widespread. Articles appeared in the New York Times,

Neue Zürcher Zeitung, El Pais, Der Spiegel, Die Zeit, Die Welt, Sueddeutsche Zeitung and elsewhere.

This essay sends a farewell to the twentieth and a welcome to the twenty-first century. A few years have passed, but the content is possibly even more relevant now. It is my hope that readers will be stimulated and moved to post comments and a few review words about the essay.

Thank you.
E.S.   May 2013

Restore my voice for me.
—Navajo

In mass societies, myth takes the place of history.
—William Bosenbrook

Mass-migratory tourism made possible by technology is now one of the world's largest industries. It began as travel, and that is what interests me: travel through space, time, experience, and the travel of ideas. It sounds straight forward enough, but a second look shows how multifaceted the notion really is. There are many different modes and manifestations of travel. Moving one's mind through cyberspace is a more recent one.

My own journey started in Weimar or thereabouts. I wasn't born there, but the city is the source of one of my earliest memories. The one and only thing I remember vividly is the image of a sunlit facade. My mother used to tell the tale about walking through town with her three year old daughter who would regularly stop in front of a particular building, point her finger, and say: *"Guck mal , Mutti, das ist das Haus der Frau von Stein."* (Look, mommy, this is the house of the Frau von Stein).

This then is about travels, and about revisiting Weimar in a roundabout way. Call it a circular movement from the past to the future, and vice versa. Call it a quest. I wonder what Goethe would say to our latest mode of transportation through electronic space?

Declaring the death of this or that is a favorite human pastime, and there is never a shortage of perennial Cassandras predicting the end of history, art, ethics, education, literature or even of civilization. It strikes me as comical now, but long ago I was also smitten by an epiphany of a similar kind: I saw the death of literacy with youthful clarity. If you love language this is not a minor matter. But as we will see later on, the news about literacy's demise was greatly exaggerated. Today, the word and the passion for writing, reading,and conversing are making an unexpected comeback. Such upcoming trends were of course completely hidden to me on the particular Sunday afternoon years ago when the message hit home: it's all over. The pessimists among the prophets are right. From now on it's going to be downhill all the way.

The location where this gloomy revelation took hold of me was Schloss Jaegerhof, a little Rococo castle at the edge of a park in the middle of the city. It was home to the Goethe Museum of the Anton and Katharina Kippenberg Stiftung. Düsseldorf's traffic sounds broke like surf pounding a cliff against the outside walls. But the noise faded soon into the background. Feeling pleasantly encapsulated by 18th century interior spaces and circulating through rooms painted in pale yellow and white, I forgot the city and spent the whole afternoon reading, unable to stop, eavesdropping on the private conversations of persons who seemed to live on a remote planet in a far-away constellation. Anthropologists have a name for the experience: code-shifting. It describes people who speak the same language but live in different worlds.

The displayed correspondence between Goethe, his friends, and his acquaintances was written in German. The handwriting presented no barrier to deciphering the content. Nevertheless, to me it was all completely alien. It had nothing to do with con-temporary life. It wasn't the kind of language used on the street, at work, in politics, in the media, in schools, or at play. It was based on different assump-tions. It was too natural and too elegant at the same time. No one talked or wrote like Goethe and his cir-cle any longer. That particular version of the Republic of Letters was indeed buried and dead.

The longer I continued reading the more I felt like a sample specimen from a society of semi-literates. I felt like a Swiftian Yahoo. I stared at these epistolary mon-uments from the past like a modern rustic who gapes at the Pyramids or the Parthenon. But simultaneously there was also an abrupt understanding that during the years when these people flourished you didn't have to be a J.W. v. G. to use language with the skill of a world class violin soloist. And you didn't have to dwell on

Mount Olympus to write and reason with the greatest ease. It came with the territory. If J.W. v. G. took up residence on the summit, fine. Let him. There was plenty of room and fresh air available for others. The views were nearly as good from many of the neighboring peaks. If you built your house high on a hill you would still be able to see across the entire mountain range while honing your sense of perspective. No doubt, all these letter writers were afflicted with an advanced case of literacy. It was nourished by the overall quality of the environment. Goethe wasn't Mr. Genius who stood utterly alone and so tall that communication with his fellows became impossible. No code-shifting occurred. Compared to these earlier practitioners of the German language we, the later arrivals, surely live with our noses rooting in the swamps.

Clearly, on that afternoon I was code-shifted. It was a discomforting sensation, and the sense of dislocation it produced has remained fresh and immediate ever since. But what was it that had been dislocated? Did I mistake social and linguistic change for discontinuity or decline? And who, for all practical purposes, cared any longer about a few Dead-White-Males and some females who wielded their ink-dipped feathers expertly two centuries ago? Perhaps this mattered to a select number of scholars and lovers of language antiquities, yet for the world and your humble servant, both of us were busily spinning on and moving forward, fast. But toward what did we travel? The sublimely passive state of becoming mere receivers of measly media transmissions? Admittedly, the word revolution has lost some of its punch by inflationary overuse and trivialization. I could use "quantum leap," or "fast forward," but that wouldn't be quite satisfactory either. So, for want of a better term, revolution will have to do. There have been three communications revolutions so far: the invention of writing, the recording of written information on tablets, scrolls, and in books, and the development of the printing press. What is happening right now is the fourth full-blown communications revolution. Nothing quite like it has occurred since Gutenberg initiated the shift from script to print.

Elizabeth Eisenstein investigated the switch "from image culture to word culture" in her massive study *The Printing Press as an Agent of Change*. She points out that the propagation of texts became practical and economical almost over night. Prior to the printing press, monastic scribes painstakingly copied books by hand. On average, a highly skilled monk could finish four pages per day, or about 1200 pages per year. Only the privileged few could afford, enjoy, or even read books – in Latin. But within fifty short years after Gutenberg's printing press started its march across Europe, a printer could out produce a cottage-industry scribe and the few fine manuscript copies he was able to make by mass-producing an edition of a thousand copies of the same text quickly and at a fraction of the cost. The price of a book plunged like the 1929 stock market on Black Tuesday. Suddenly the average sixteenth century buyer had to work only an hour or two before he was able to pay for a book. And if he couldn't read, he now had incentives to learn. One thing led to another. Soon, books were available not only in Latin, but also in vernacular languages. Martin Luther's German Bible was immediately within the reach of the common man. And by acquiring the skill of reading for himself, the adult student was freed, at least to a large extent, from the teacher who was usually a member of the clergy. Side-effects of this were the loosening of ties to established authority and a new awareness of the individual.

As we have seen, the rapid success of printing led to a multiplication of texts and of access to printed materials. This in turn influenced the oral traditions. The book became a common storage container for information, and as a result the older mnemonic aids of rhyme and cadence lost their importance. The ancient Celts had storytellers who, it is said, could recite 350 full-length epics by heart. But what was formerly preserved in the brain was now widely available from the printed page. Even the visual art that had once been reserved for churches and the palaces of nobles could be reproduced in the illustrations that were added to printed books.

N. Scott Momaday, the first Native American author to win the Pulitzer Prize, has re-lived the formidable jump from oral to written expression in our time. In *The Man Made of Words* (1997), he speaks beautifully about it. To him, who is part of it and lived on an Indian Reservation, the oral tradition of the American Indian is based on the "deep and unconditional belief in the efficacy of language. Words are intrinsically powerful. They are magical. By means of words one can bring about physical change in the universe. By means of words can one quiet the weather, bring forth the harvest, ward off evil, rid the body of sickness and pain, subdue an enemy, capture the heart of a lover, and venture forth beyond death." Momaday's work, which I discovered years after leaving Germany, echoes the experience that the letters of Goethe and his circle had left in my mind.

In the Europe of the 16th century it was no longer the oral message but the newly printed word that traveled like wildfire while spreading knowledge. Elizabeth Eisenstein argues that the reduction in the costs of books made the Reformation possible. Without printing technology, the effective propagation of Luther's and Calvin's heresies would have been suppressed: such irregularities were usually silenced in time-honored fashion. But mass-produced books and pamphlets, translated from Latin into German and other vernacular languages, delivered the power of words to everyone, and made them irrepressible. In addition, the printing press became the means for distributing material on scientific ideas and methods, and the catalyst for forming subcultures of authors, intellectuals, and scientists. Before long the printer's shop functioned as the favorite gathering place for scholars, writers, and artists. When growth called for grander arrangements, Frankfurt am Main – which is still the location for the world's biggest annual book fair – evolved as a central market place for the publishing trade. Old fair catalogs and city records survive. They tell us how much it cost to print a *Ballen* of paper consisting of twelve *Ries* with forty sheets each, and that a single press could print up to one hundred Ballen of paper per year. They also show how exploding demand led to a rapid expansion in paper-making capacity: by 1500, there were already about fifty paper mills in Germany. The number and location of the mills was limited by the size and affluence of the population. Rags were the raw material for paper-making and only reasonably well-off citizens could afford to discard their old textiles regularly.

Frankfurt developed not only as a central market for books and the publishing business; it also served as a stock exchange for the trade in ideas.

No matter how diligently the Holy Office in Rome busied itself to uphold censorship, prohibited books were cheerfully smuggled across the Alps and into Italy's cities. To ensure success, the bookmen affixed false title pages and colophons, bribed customs officials, and frustrated the Inquisition's efforts to stop the influx of black-listed texts into Italy, or the export of daring manuscripts out of it.

Yet the exuberance, the unfettered wheeling and dealing during the initial period of the printing revolution, eventually encountered stifling trends. The political and religious climate changed in large parts of Europe, and except for a scientific oasis here and there, especially in England and the Low Countries, a little intellectual ice age began. Before long the Thirty Years' War cut a swath of destruction across Central Europe. The book trade was seriously harmed, and with it the printers and authors. An appointed Imperial Book Commission (*Kaiserliche Buecherkommission*) tried to turn the clock back even more. Hounding the Frankfurt Book Fairs, Vienna's civil servants attempted to regulate, censor, prohibit, and control publishing.

In the long run, however, attempts to have power over the free flow of information didn't work. Ideas, not unlike bacteria and viruses, tend to be survivors. No matter how much we try to win the contest against them, and no matter how rigorously we proceed, they always seem to be one step ahead in the race, metamorphosing and adapting as necessary – and ultimately arriving first. Printing continued to expand, sending ideas on journeys across the opening world, with presses springing up as far away as Guatemala, all the while leaving traces, planting seeds, making contact with minds from other cultures. It was a dynamic process, and by the 18th and early 19th centuries Europeans had taken up the passion to explore, find, collect, translate, and understand the literary treasures and lore of far-away lands. The passionate Orientalist's (not yet a term of ill repute) mentality flourished: Friedrich Schlegel published his pioneering *On the Language and Wisdom of the East Indians* (1808), his brother August Wilhelm was the first professor of Sanskrit in Bonn, Hammer-Purgstall translated the Persian poet Hafiz (1812), and Goethe wrote his *Westöstlicher Divan* (1819). Almost simultaneously the genre of travel literature came into its own, bringing the far reaches of the world and exotic tales of adventure, hardship, and endurance to the comfort of armchair travelers at home. The delightful letters (1717-1718) of Lady Mary Wortley Montagu, wife of the British ambassador to the Sublime Porte, are but one early example, although in her case without the necessity of roughing it. Painting vivid portraits of life in Istanbul, (or Constantinople as habit still named the city) the lady even managed to visit the royal harem. She reported on it in the most intricate and amusing detail.

How much things have changed in the second half of the 20th century! Travelers became tourists who now cross the earth by flying, sailing, or driving along on primarily pre-selected tracks. The evolution of film, television, video, and the electronic media inundates us with pictures: it has made voyeurs of us all. Is there a man, woman, or child with a TV set or personal computer nearby, even if it is the only one in a remote village at the end of the earth, who hasn't seen the Grand Canyon, the Eiffel Tower, Donald Duck, Coca Cola commercials, or the Space Station on a screen?

Trade, messages, and people are now being blown across the globe in a never-ending motion, taking hold here and there, or simply circulating like the space debris we have left orbiting in earth's stratosphere. What for? Is it useful? What does it accomplish? Have we finally learned how to talk to our neighbors? Are we less intolerant? And if not, why not? Has all this broadcasting, navigating, steering, and traveling consequences, and if so why do we hear so many trumpet sounds about the up-and-coming clash of civilizations?

Actually, many tourists do not change their outlook merely by being transported from Germany to a beach in Spain, or from the US to a beach in Costa Rica or the Caribbean. Prejudices tend to travel with the baggage, and if not lost in transit, the same bags, enlarged by a few souvenirs, can return in the identical unshaken condition. Business travelers are also shielded and protected against culture shock by the internationally standardized comforts and trappings of the airport, corporate, and hotel environments.

Time to stand still now, for just a moment. Time to take a slow breath, recalling the afternoon spent with Goethe's correspondence, when it seemed that literacy had grown comatose. Of course years later people are still complaining about the same thing. And it is true that there is a particular dumbing down, definitely in the US, but also, if one listens to critics, in Europe. Moreover, it's now a cliché to say that we have too much information and too little time. What good is information if we can't turn it into knowledge? Furthermore, many of us have been demoted to function as an audience whether we like it or not. We became specimens of passivity, almost as hapless as butterflies or beetles that someone pinned to a cardboard with a needle. That's the way we were, and

still are: collectibles, statistics, samples of the species, nicely numbed for classification and study.

Mass communications and the mass media have
treated us casually as a nameless crowd, categorized
at best by demographics, zip codes, voting patterns,
and habits of consumption. It's not exactly flattering.
We are told what is in and what is out. Labels are
affixed to us, marking us as blue collar workers, white
collar workers, upscale consumers, part-timers, plat-
inum card holders, Joe-six-pack types, baby boom-
ers, and generation Xers – whatever. There are
countless books on how to handle us, how to push
our buttons, how to engineer consent among us, and
how to master and manipulate the symbols that are
dear to our hearts.

I am not certain when these methods of species
management through PR, communications, and the
mass media began, but the basic concepts were available as early as the turn of the century. In 1898,
Gabriel Tarde observed that people who didn't read
the newspapers were influenced by those who did
and talked about it. Thus, he said in *On Opinion and
Conversation*, "the non-readers are forced to follow
the grove of their borrowed thoughts. . . One pen suf-
fices to set off a million tongues." By 1920, Everett
Dean Martin, author of *The Behavior of Crowds*, saw
the possibilities of managing large numbers of people with far more ambition. He wrote that we "must
become a cult, write our philosophy of life in flaming
headlines, and sell our cause in the market. No

matter if we meanwhile surrender every value for which we stand, we must strive to cajole the majority into imagining itself on our side. . . It is numbers that count – quantity, not quality."

What impact did such programs of persuasion have on the western democracies? If N. Scott Momaday is right in saying – and I think he is – that words are powerful, magical, and that they can "bring about physical change in the universe," then those 1920 writings by Everett Dean Martin sound not only visionary, but also frightening. The history of the 20th century seems to confirm him. Many of us, and many of our fathers and grandfathers, and not only those who had to exist under totalitarian systems, can recall when radio, newspapers, film, and television became potent tools in the attempt to manipulate the public. Initially the newness of the mass media was matched by a certain innocence and credulity of the listeners and viewers. People were not yet sophisticated about the technology. They were more trusting, and not at all cynical towards the tricks of the trade. And initially, the media may have approached audiences likewise with the best of intentions.

Back then, no educator would have dreamed of developing courses in "media literacy" for schools. But here and there, we can now find a few of such courses. They aim to prepare the young for the onslaught of information and imagery by teaching how to ask critical questions. They point to the manipulation of expectations, and encourage the search for fact and for truth. Children can learn to detect the differences between public relations, stacked news, and the fine art of omissions. To the country, and perhaps to the world, the subject matter offered by the mainstream media, the unctuous style, and the hair-splitting content may often be as relevant as weather reports from Mars. There is a *disconnect* between the press corps and the public, and back in the October 1998 issue of Brill's Content, a media watch publication that's now defunct , a whopping 48 percent of newspaper editors and publishers said that news coverage is shallow and inadequate. Imagine having to work under such conditions, and consider how much worse it grows day by day.

But back then as technology changed, competition increased, viewers grew more experienced, the audience began to fracture, and to decline, at least in the US. In big city markets, or for those who installed their own small dish antenna, hundreds of cable channels became available. But viewing time did not increase. To the contrary, it decreased because Americans were asked to raise productivity by working longer hours, mostly without increases in pay. Everybody you run into seems to be harassed. The quality of media content did not improve either. Cheap talk shows and reruns of old programming and movies proliferated. Standards and taste reached new lows.

Critics say that a modern democracy can not function without having informed citizens and freedom of the press. Yet the quality in the mainstream media is declining steadily. In fact, during a panel discussion at the new American Academy in Berlin (shown on the non-commercial U.S. TV channel C-Span in August 1998) participants, among them Fritz Stern of Columbia University, Richard von Weizsaecker, and the German film maker Volker Schloendorff, heard the term 'totalitarian entertainment' to describe the programming offered by media moguls. The panelists wondered, somewhat tongue-in-cheek, how one can guarantee freedom in programming when a small number of dominant people and corporate conglomerates control what the public in democratic countries will see and hear.

Media self-criticism, at least out in the open, is a fairly new phenomenon of the last few years. In December of 1995, Andrew Lack, president of NBC News, said that we "are spawning a generation of reporters and news directors who no longer place any value on the written word, the turn of the phrase, the uncut, long, hard question. All we care about are the almighty pictures, the video, the story count - and that it moves like a bat out of hell. We barely listen to what is said anymore."

That comment was made years ago, and since then things have heated up. The journalism profession now behaves somewhat frantically. It misses few opportunities to warn the public about the dangers of the Internet for children, potential victims of scams or terrorism, and gullible souls. It pens Luddite warnings about the ghost in the machine and the trashiness of the electronic word. It assures itself that world affairs would come to a standstill without the punditry and interpretations offered by professionals, and at the same time it bemoans incidents of coverage in respectable publications that slide down to the level of the gutter press. The mainstream media like to believe that the average citizen, like the average burgher during the Gutenberg revolution, requires guidance and explanation from the elevated vantage point of the bully pulpit or the news desk. Perhaps journalists try to calm their own anxieties by speculating that America is for Dummies (the name of one book among many "Dummy" titles).

There is less complacency. Conferences and columns now deal with the deterioration of the field or recall, somewhat ruefully, that yellow journalism is nothing new. In a famous incident prior to the Spanish-American War, press magnate William Randolph Hearst assigned the artist Frederic Remington to Havana. Bored in Cuba, Remington cabled to his employer: "Everything is quiet. There is no trouble here. There will be no war. I wish to return." Hearst cabled back: "Please remain. You furnish the pictures, and I'll furnish the war." The press baron, using his newspapers, set out to fulfill the prophecy: he got his war.

Today's reporters and columnists are put under pressure to deliver details that can help in beating the competition. A few of the journalists succumb by delivering what is not there: invented stories or quotes, sources without attribution, and material that has been spiced up and made sexy with a bit of fiction. When fabrications were discovered heads began to roll, for example in 1998 at The New Republic and the Boston Globe. But that the problem is more systemic becomes clearer when a prestigious journal like the Harvard Business Review finds it necessary to alert readers to new books with titles like *News and the Culture of Lying; Who Stole the News: Why We Can't Keep up with What Happens in the World;* and *Tainted Truth: The Manipulation of Fact in America.*

The news actually contains less and less news and more and more infotainment at a time when viewership of the national network news has fallen from 60 percent in 1993 to 38 percent of Americans in 1998. America is turning away and tuning out. The situation is still somewhat better for newspapers. But the faithful readers are mostly mature adults and seniors. Overall, the young have little interest in reading the papers.

These developments during the second half of the 20th century signify nothing less than a reversal of the Gutenberg revolution. If, as stated by Elizabeth Eisenstein, the printing press facilitated the progression from "image culture to word culture, " then our mass media age turned this on its head and marched us, willingly or not, from the word culture straight back to the image culture. In fact we moved in reverse toward a pre-Enlightenment world, back to the womb, and to our own Ersatz-versions of faith. During the Middle Ages, great religious art was created and displayed in churches for the benefit of believers who could not read. But who were the believers of the television age, and what was displayed to them? What did they see or perceive? Which icons? Which images? What family of symbols, emblems and pictorial messages? What truth, semi-truth, or untruth? What Ersatz? And what if it is true that a one-sided visual diet of television and movies diminishes the ability to think and reason? And that it favors instinct and emotion?

Abstract thinking, rhetoric, and literate ways of relating to the world were traditionally the domain of the educated elites. Thanks to universal education the majority has long learned to write and read, yet it may still come to prefer pictures and the spoken, instead of the written word. At certain points in history the hierarchical relationships undergo change, and the idea to provide schooling for all children, and to educate future workers so that they can become productive citizens of post-agricultural, industrialized, or technological societies was one of these changes. Still, the urge of the few to control and persuade the many seems to transmogrify itself time and again, repackaging and renaming itself, dressing its aims in the latest ideological and social fashions, which may or may not resemble the Emperor's New Clothes. I think that such efforts are part of the human condition and that they will be found under any form of government, even in the western democracies.

But then, seemingly just at the right historic moment, another massive shift of the tectonic plates occurred: the Internet came to the surface of the public mind. In 1996, personal computer sales outpaced TV sales for the second year in succession. And regardless of the hype and hoopla generated in its wake, the new kid on the electronic block learned to speak for itself within a few short years. The material available online doubled every eight months, and much of it was valuable information from the world's leading universities, libraries, and institutions. In fact, the Internet and its younger brother, the Web, grew so fast that by mid-1998 America Online was worth three times as much as the big American networks of ABC, CBS, and NBC combined. And Yahoo, a Web browser/guide started by Stanford graduate students David Filo and Jerry Yang as a personal Internet filing system in 1994, financially surpassed the value – at least as long as the stock market runs with the bulls – of the venerable old battleship of the print media, the New York Times.

If we disregard a few detours, a clearly delineated course emerges. It leads from the 16th century dissemination of printed words to 20th century digital travel through cyberspace. The computer is doing for us what the printing press did for the people of the Renaissance and the Reformation: it sets us free from being passive members of audience-dom, and it is a tool for dealing with complexity and ever increasing amounts of human knowledge. (There aren't enough trees on earth to print, on paper, what is out there). The now widely used prefix "cyber" is an apt one: it derives from the Greek word *Kubernetes*, meaning steersman. Norbert Wiener coined "cybernetics" for communications theory in 1954, and the term cyberspace was first used in 1984 by the science fiction writer William Gibson. Cyber is now being tagged onto everything from punk to soul to chic.

Of course the metaphor of navigating and steering not only implies movement through electronic space but also through physical space, and indeed, discovery by sea and land led the way. Many of the technological advances of the last five hundred were related to transportation. They enabled us to move goods, people, and equipment with greater ease, lower costs, increasing speed, and in ever larger numbers. First came ships and voyages of exploration, then rail roads, cars, long distance freeways, airplanes, a moon landing, container ships, air travel for millions of passengers, and finally satellites, radio telescopes, a space station, the space shuttle, and space probes. That so much transportation causes large amounts of pollution is another matter.

First we had printing, then the telegraph, the telephone, broadcasting (an agricultural term used since the 1760's or 1770's. It stands for the dispersing of seeds), television, video, the computer, and eventually electronic communications via the Internet. So here we are, using computers as our ships, sailing across the continents almost as swiftly as thought.

"*Die Gedanken sind frei*" (thoughts are free) we used to sing as children. How could I have dreamed about a technology, or a magic, that could do just that: transport written thoughts in an instant over great distances? The wonder and the freedom of it strike me daily.

During the Gutenberg revolution more people learned to read so that they could deal with the content of books independently and without intermediaries. Today, a similar process repeats itself. A rapidly growing number of individuals select to bypass the middlemen and gatekeepers of the mainstream media. In 1996, six percent of Americans retrieved news from the Internet. Now, only two years later, twenty percent do. They pick what they want to read during their scarce free time, cross borders in seconds, and become acquainted with a variety of viewpoints if they wish to do so. People who received information exclusively from a national press are now exposed to transnational perspectives unless they live in a politically repressed country or with their own apathy. For those who are free and willing to roam, catching news on the net is easy. And why wait if you can custom-tailor your selections according to your own interests? Why wait or rely on the often paltry coverage offered by the television networks, cable TV, or most of the press?

Both television and newspapers, with the exception of the largest and the chain-owning corporations, have closed foreign offices and cut the number of correspondents to save costs. This works like a self-fulfilling prophecy: declining readership and advertising revenues cause belt tightening, which leads to less interesting content, which drives even more well educated and relatively affluent readers to the Internet for news. Editors at most papers use the same wire services. Before long, a landscape of conformity unfolds. Only the local coverage differs, while the range of reporting grows ever more narrow and provincial.

The shift of the informational tectonic plates is well documented by the advertising television and newspapers do for their own Internet pages and email addresses. Invitations to visit online for updates and greater details are now a routine. Responses are solicited. "Talk to us", my daily newspaper pleads. "E-mail us at access.nameofpaper.com with your comments, suggestions, and questions." All these media efforts try to hold on to the paying customer. They occur in competition with a gigantic flow of free-of-charge materials offered online, and in competition for the attention of individuals who have only a fixed or even shrinking amount of personal time at their disposal. Demands on personal time increase ever more, urging: stay healthy - exercise! Spend more time with your children! Help them with homework! Find quiet time for yourself! Volunteer! Enroll in computer classes! Finish your MBA on weekends! Work overtime without grumbling! Don't be a workaholic! Take up Yoga – meditate for peace of mind, etc. etc. All these conflicting imperatives often screech like sound bites from a play given in the Theater of the Absurd.

Nonetheless, the volume of information on the Net multiplies almost exponentially and has already grown to more than 320 million web pages worldwide. Many of these sites are either amateurish or commercial, but even more of them are excellent, ranging from sophisticated pages maintained by the Library of Congress, the world's top museums, and major universities, to profiles of practically every city on earth. One can spend hours exploring just one of these big sites, and days in following the links to other locations. It works almost like a spaceship's jump through hyperspace in a special effects movie. Just click, and split seconds later you are at your destination. You can visit many countries. You can fly through the planetary system or to distant galaxies, check up on Galileo's work on the phases of the moon, find primary documents of world history or human rights records, do research in major libraries, shop online for books, trips, and airline tickets, or find reliable details on health conditions and treatments which you can then present as clues to your hard pressed, time-starved physician. Thirty-four million Americans already log on and use the Internet as a medical library because their doctors can't talk to them due to demands for cost-control and efficiency. Yet in the end, the single day of an information-drenched human being still has only 24 hours, most of which will be spent working, driving, living, loving, eating, and sleeping.

I have heard it said that democracy stops every morning as soon as the average citizen arrives at his or her place of employment. Maybe that's putting it a bit too harshly, but it certainly contains grains of truth. The majority earns a living by doing the job it was hired to do. Communications while working are, to a degree, a carefully staged, and smartly choreo- graphed dance in the art of being well deceived. What employees say can make or break them. They play office politics at their own risk, speak out at their own risk, and gossip at their own risk. So most working stiffs should probably ignore the career-related how- to-books of the season, and catch up on the ancient skills of Renard the Fox instead. The point is that even at work, which occupies the largest portion of our waking hours, communication isn't open or freely democratic.

So when do people talk? Seriously, honestly, and with irreverence? Where are our public places? Where, as citizens, can we test our mettle and debate with wit and passion? Must we step on a soap box and orate on a street corner in New York's Soho? Should we start a new cafe society? A salon? The forum? Yes, we should do all of the above. The func- tioning of democracy and the participation of its citi- zens worldwide may depend on it. Fortunately, it has already happened: the Internet can be, at best, the new incarnation of the literary and political salon , of the forum of antiquity, of skid row, and of other pub- lic places high and low. The forms and conventions have changed, but the basic functions remain the

same: these are social places where citizens can inter-
act, discuss, debate, and engage in verbal fights.
(Shouting is less dangerous than shooting). During
the decades when mass media dominance was at its
peak, public meeting grounds had practically disappeared. They were replaced by interest groups, which
is not the same thing. David Riesman's 1950's por-
trait of Americans as *The Lonely Crowd* reflects an
uncanny mirror image of the media consumer,
stranded with his nuclear family or even alone in a
living room, and insulated from the real world at
large.

The current communications revolution started
when some inventive and pleasantly garrulous scientists grew tired of various restrictions and set out to
circumvent them, first for themselves, and eventually, perhaps inadvertently, for the rest of us. In the
process they demilitarized the Internet, which had
been the APRAnet (Advanced Research Projects
Agency network) of the US Department of Defense.
The mindset of national defense and the mindset of
information technology soon clashed ideologically.
The first was dedicated to controlling military information; the second depended on the opposite, namely
the free flow of bits and bytes. To find a way out of
the dilemma, computer scientists started their own
parallel communications network in 1979. It was the
birth year of Usenet News, and it soon grew into the
fledgling Internet. The intellectual independence
and open atmosphere of the early Usenet set the tone
for things to come. There are now 30,000 public

places in cyberspace where people from around the world drop in for Usenet discussions on a multitude of topics from silly to serious. Within these gathering spots, dialogue becomes polylogue. So far, Usenet represents the social side of the information revolution, and who knows what else will evolve later on. For now, this is our printer's shop, our marketplace of ideas, our agora, our equivalent of the 16th century Frankfurt Book Fair, our debating society, our meeting place of minds. And perhaps, if more people with experience, good sense, and expert knowledge emerge from their Ivory Towers and from their solitary pursuits of private scholarship and decide to participate, we can resurrect an electronic version of the Republic of Letters. But does this mean that all is currently well in the best of all worlds?

Not really. I get goose bumps from listening to a gallery of frequently youthful testosterone-driven Wall Streeters, investment bankers, and we-know-how-to-fix-it-all types expound day in day out on the world economy while lecturing other countries on how to make sacrifices. I somehow doubt that these dashing Masters of the Universe (as Tom Wolfe has named them) know what a sacrifice is. And as I write this, our semi-McLuhanesque global village finds itself shaken by a destabilizing economic turbulence. Stock markets have plunged or follow a roller coaster zigzag course. Hedge funds stumble. Currencies lost value. Russia is threatened by an economic and political meltdown. Some Asian and Latin American economies are under siege. Several countries are beginning to doubt the free financial market orthodoxy. The volatile ebb and tide of huge sums of short term money rushing in and out of the so-called emerging markets is being named as one of the causes for the latest popular delusions and the madness of crowds. Indonesians riot, Kosovo flees, the Congo bleeds, terrorists bomb, and the U.S. counter-bombs. And as if wanting to add misery to the human cacophony, rivers flood, wildfires burn, storms eat beaches, and droughts devour crops. The other day I saw an unusual employment advertisement in the 26 Sept. 1998 issue of the *Economist*: The World Bank seeks a Poverty Economist. At first glance this looked like an oxymoron, but on second thought it was an emblem, or a shorthand message that tells much in a nutshell.

By the same token, just because economic, technological, and pop-cultural forces seem to pull the world together in a process of globalization, one shouldn't assume that poverty, conflict, and long-term problems can be smoothed over. We are still divided into the rich and the poor. A crisis in world financial markets can still plunge tens of millions into hardship and renewed poverty. And the Cold War is barely over, so how can we overlook that it kept an artificial atomic lid on the ferment of peoples and societies? The turmoil was there even if it disappeared for a while, like a river that goes underground. There it runs, carving its path below the Karst, gushing over rocks, keeping its course. And what about the process of post-World War II decolonization? How can it be over so fast? Was there enough time to sort things out before the Cold War, the East-West standoff, and the division of the world into two major spheres of influence interrupted something that had barely begun? If colonization was a process that required several centuries and came gradually to an end after 1945, or, in some ways, only after 1990, how can one expect that the newly independent countries achieve their difficult balance in only a few decades or after a few years? There can be no doubt that much of the world was changed during its blending with major powers.

It would be a practical impossibility, for example, to overlook the Spanish imprint on large parts of the Americas or even on the American Southwest, where 1998 marks the (not uncontested) celebration of the *Cuarto Centenario*, the 400th anniversary of Spanish settlement north of the Rio Grande. In 1598, years before the first English pilgrims came ashore at Plymouth Rock, Don Juan de Onate took formal possession of what is now New Mexico and Arizona for the Spanish crown. With Onate came two hundred settlers, their families, livestock, and a rich supply of seeds, humble messengers of strong cultural contact. And this year, Onate's and his settlers' direct descendants, together with visiting Spanish officials gathered in Santa Fe to commemorate the event. The annual Fiesta was especially exuberant in honor of the anniversary.

I live along the Rio Grande, in a region that contains the oldest architectural artifacts on the North

American continent: Chaco Canyon's cities were built when Europe began to erect its Gothic cathedrals. These finely crafted stone apartments of the Pre-Columbian Anasazi culture (a Navajo word, meaning "the Ancient Ones", or, less polite, the "Ancient Enemies") with their Great Houses and round ceremonial Kiva rooms were abandoned before the first Europeans arrived. The reasons for the exodus of these architects, road builders, astronomers, engineers, artists, and agriculturists are not entirely clear to this day.

The expansive parcel of land called New Mexico also contains Trinity Site, located in a stretch of harsh desert one had to cross when traveling north on the Camino Real from Mexico, which was back then the Kingdom of New Spain. The Spaniards who came along the Royal Road couldn't know that the first atomic bomb would be exploded in this desert centuries later, yet in an ironic twist of fate they named it fittingly: *Jornada del Muerto.* Not too far from Trinity, on a remote fossil-bearing plateau called the Plains of San Agustin stands another marvel of the 20th century: a congregation of giant ears. They listen to the universe. Here, scientists collect radio waves from stars, galaxies, and, since March of 1998, bursts of gamma rays which suggest the explosion of a " hypernova," a huge blast that may turn a single star into a black hole. What was a shallow lake bed during the last ice age 12,000 years ago now hosts one of the world's largest radio telescopes, the Karl J. Jansky Very Large Array. Each of the 27 telescopes has a diameter of 82 feet, is 94 feet tall, weighs 235 tons, and moves on tracks that form a huge Y. The 27 antennas work in unison. Their combined power equals that of a single telescope with a diameter of 17 miles. Cattle graze peacefully around the steel-footed giants.

To heighten the contrasts further, a short drive brings the traveler from the high-tech radio telescopes to the once booming and now sleepy cow town of Magdalena at Trail's End –which today it truly is. Yet from the 1880's to the 1920's, cattle drives ended here, ready to meet a little railroad which carried the livestock to the East Coast. Yet another leap across some miles and a range of the Gila mountains transports the traveler to the ancient home of the Mimbres people who, between 1000 and 1150 A.D., created pottery with stunningly black-on-white abstract designs that would have delighted a Kandinsky or a Miro.

In a land such as this the very old and the very new exist side by side. It is a partly semi-arid, and partly wild, green, and mountainous region that depends on scarce life-sustaining water and thereby imposes limits on population growth. For that reason the cultural landscapes of past and future are not covered up, veiled, or overgrown by the conglomerations of contemporary life like in the big cities. The geological and the human strata remain visible. Living in such surroundings tends to sharpen one's sense of perspective and of paradox. This is a place of divergent cosmologies, histories, languages, educations, purposes, and perceptions. For example: Benjamin Whorf, who studied the Hopi language and pointed to a still contentious theory of knowledge while doing so, illustrated how languages shape people's ideas and thoughts. The gap between a European language and Hopi is incredibly great. What is interesting, however, is Whorf's data indicate that the Hopi way of talking has a natural affinity with the most complex theories of modern physics. To a Hopi, quantum mechanics and the space-time continuum are understandable. He has the linguistic and therefore perceptive equipment to grasp such concepts with ease.

Filled with such baffling surprises, it is no wonder that this region can be seen as a proving ground for cultural coexistence and for finding out what makes all of us tick: Hopis and Navajos, Zunis and Acomas, native people living in the age-old Rio Grande pueblos, Spaniards living in remote mountain villages as they have for centuries, Americans, Asians, Blacks, and new immigrants from Mexico and Central America. To me, this portion of the United States is like a scale model of the larger world. In a very concrete way globalism begins here, at the local level. I am fond of this land and its diverse inhabitants. It has taught me, by example, that cultures are stubborn, and not essentially rational. They can mix and mingle for centuries, yet their own characteristics hang on, and even thrive. And why not? (I have also seen the opposite: extreme cultural dislocation and the destruction of the crutches of meaning, and it is heart-breaking). Here I can observe how long it takes to walk a few steps forward, or backwards, or roundabout, despite all the sophisticated high-tech brainpower and equipment that dazzles us. And while some of the Indian nations have business acumen and send a few of their children to study law or electrical engineering, others live with conditions that match those found in the Third World.

It is this daily observed reality that causes me to distrust short cuts and quick fixes. It took a long time for the European Union to arrive at the current limited level of integration, and much more work remains to be done, particularly among its own citizens. It was a process based on intelligent compromise and on horse trading, not on revolution. Still, when times turn difficult and unemployment rises, societies and individuals tend to withdraw their feelers and shrink inwards like snails into their shell.

With the Cold War barely behind us, it is perhaps understandable that geopolitical monuments like Samuel P. Huntington's *The Clash of Civilizations and the Remaking of World Order*, or Francis Fukuyama's *The End of History* make someone like me (with a central-European experience) uncomfortable. The first work encourages the West to pull together, warns about possible decline (an old Jeremiad a la Spengler), and wishes to prepare Westerners (which Westerners?) for the newest round of us against them. The second work is a bit too optimistic for my history-soaked old world memories in its assumption that the race for the global victory of liberal democracy has already been won, and that we can now live happily ever after under the evenly distributed sunshine of capitalism. This makes me think of Russia's unpaid workers, of 1.1 billion or more people who live on a dollar a day, and of many other unlovely realities. Yes, the much-talked about movement toward a global market is shaping up: the car I drive is a genuine transnational product – many of its components are made in different countries by people speaking different languages. But clearly, such a convergence can't be based on short-term good-weather cycles only, nor can it be facilitated by drafting the next evil empire or civilization into the handwriting on the wall. It is only when Samuel Huntington argues that "what is universalism to the West, is imperialism to the rest," that I am willing to take his word for it. This may indeed be the perception of many who look from the outside in.

Since social changes always take longer than expected, no dashing thesis will lessen the necessity of dealing reasonably and incrementally with the strong yet understandable tension between globalism and tribalism in all its old or newfangled forms. Culture, ethnicity, religion, nationalism, regionalism, clan, or family seem to be manifestations of the inherent human desire that seeks to belong. "Roots precede routes," says the anthropologist James

Clifford, reporting on the field work of Indian eth-
nographer Amitav Gosh who studied the long-term
travel and migration habits of villagers in Egypt.
"Everyone is on the move," Gosh wrote, "and has
been for centuries." And it is from these roots that
the travelers and migrants venture out, carrying their
cultural luggage with them like portable goods,
bringing it back on their return, or setting it down at
a new place of dwelling. What I don't understand or
accept is the necessity of seeing two aspects of one
reality strictly as opposites. Why can't they comple-
ment each other? Why can't they meet and borrow
what is useful, as they have done it since antiquity?
And why can't we look at the world based on two different optical magnitudes: one of them telescopic,
and the other one microscopic? One of them global,
or universal, and the other one local? We are still
dealing with same object – with a ridiculously small
planet, are we not?

Within the *Wahlheimat* and scale model of the
larger world where I have come to live, there is yet
another item of curiosity and interest: it's a way to
do science which found a home at the Santa Fe
Institute. Here, in a pristine setting with a view over
the hills and mountains of northern New Mexico,
Nobel laureates and scientists from a range of disci-
plines and countries search for the laws of complexity. Stuart Kauffman, a MacArthur Fellow and
pioneer of the emerging science as applied to biology
writes that it is "a close cousin of the recent remarkable findings. . . .physicists call self-organized

criticality. " Kauffman, who published a book titled *At Home in the Universe: The Search for the Laws of Self-Organization and Complexity*, describes this concept of nature as "order for free." Arising spontaneously, "the poised edge of chaos is a remarkable place... General laws....may govern coevolving communities of species, technologies, and even ideologies." Chaos theory (its popularized name) may also provide insights into the dynamics of economic and cultural systems, and into the rise and fall of civilizations. In contrast to geopolitical fortune tellers, Kauffman thinks that "at this poised state between order and chaos, the players cannot foretell the unfolding consequences of their actions." So as we enter a new millennium he looks for understanding, not for power. Other writers on complexity credit Immanuel Kant with catching an early glimpse into the future with its still hidden aspects of science when he said: "God has put a secret art into the forces of Nature so as to enable it to fashion itself out of chaos into a perfect world system."

If you go hunting for the laws of complexity you need powerful computers, so in Kant's time even his extraordinary mind would have been unable to find or decipher something like the language of complexity. That's a challenge that tantalizes a later born German, Mario Markus of the Max Planck Institute in Dortmund, who, with the help of computer graphics, displays almost a million variations, all nonlinear equations, and all of them possibilities for one limited aspect of nature.

Nonlinearity is one of the main elements of complexity. A year ago I saw a documentary film made of computer graphics based on Benoit Mandelbrot's fractals, and it displayed an exquisite fluid poetry of pattern making. It was complexity made visible, made flesh, made color. It was a dance of dimensions and structures, more graceful and inventive than anything witnessed before. Man is a pattern maker, too. Scientists think that the brain with its plasticity of a thousand million millions in neural connections may work in this manner. Wow. This suits me well. I would like to have a brain like that, and a mind that builds and perceives connections. In any event, computer graphics are a blessing for those of us who completely lack advanced mathematical training. It enables us to see science, and it is a valuable and innovative use of the visual.

It is interesting to note that even business leaders are beginning to pay some attention to these frontiers in science. Linear and mathematical simplicity tends to clash with the often unexpected ways in which economies work in the real world. And so, in a telecast from the February 1998 World Economic Forum in Davos, Switzerland, one could listen to speakers (on noncommercial C-Span, where else) who told the movers and shakers of international business that they will have to deal with complex systems and turbulences in the 21st century. Some of these ideas sounded as if they came straight from the Santa Fe Institute.

In *Corelli's Mandolin*, novelist Louis de Bernieres crafted a charming tongue-in-cheek paragraph about

one of our century's utopias. It reads like this, caps
and all:

"The tragedy was that this was yet another
step along the fated path by which Communism
was growing into the Greatest and Most Humane
Ideology Never to have been Implemented Even
When it Was in Power, or perhaps The Most
Noble Ever to Attract The Highest Proportion of
Hooligans and Opportunists."

Indeed, it requires grace to touch upon this, and
other vast and gory utopias of our century, with a
sense of humor. Bernieres' tone goes well with my
own allergic reaction toward any arrogant old or new
utopian schemes. I think we are better off with being
sensible, and with settling down to the nitty-gritty of
useful work: perhaps it wouldn't be such a bad idea
to recall our mothers, the long forgotten *Truemmer-
Frauen*, and how they did what had to be done, no
matter how hard it was to be stranded within a moon-
scape of rubble. Is this what self-organizing chaos
looks like? Does it begin to form order just as it did
when these haggard, hungry, exhausted women
started to deal with it? When they labored like chain-
gangs to make a dent of removal in a desert of bro-
kenness with their bare hands?

In any case, I am ready for an approach that is
modest, and yet far bolder, and far more mindful of
humans. And a new respect for the law of unintended
results would be refreshing indeed. Why force life

into another straight jacket? They will come, all the contradictions and juxtapositions, but shield me from the one-dimensional and the mono-cultural. There are so many questions we must ask. Why, for example, should it be necessary to look at the interaction between social customs and economies, and at the changes and diffusions that occur through contact between civilizations, mostly in terms of a power struggle that was far more fitting for the mindset of the 19th century and the oh-so-imperative survival of the fittest? (It is funny, but the fittest, according to Stephen Gould, are the lowly bacteria, and not humans). Isn't it feasible to outgrow such confrontational ways not because we are pure pacifists, but because anything else is unintelligent?

Yes, I do take my democracy and my pluralism seriously. And no, I am not disinclined to take a good look at the deconstructing labor of the postmodernists. Their task is mostly done. They restored a comic vision to our ideology-ridden misunderstandings, nurtured the subversive impulse against a dominating culture, used discursive slapstick, and exposed the foibles of prescribed history. (*Lies my Teacher Told Me: Everything Your American History Textbook Got Wrong* is the title of a 1995 book by James Loewen. It sold a quarter-million of copies). The new postmodern kid on the block arranged a good, vigorous house-cleaning: busts of great men were dusted off, and cob-webs were torn down. And when that was accomplished, postmodernism conjured itself into the corner of a cousin: it joined

Romantic Irony. Like the German Romanticism of the late 18th and early 19th century, in the end it too was fond of lifting the veil from the illusions it had spun. Now it sits in its corner, a little out of steam, probably laughing, and watching to see what comes along to rock the boat in the next fresh millennium.

Abstraction, if followed logically to the end, eventually leads the painter to the famous empty canvas. Similarly, the postmodern deconstructionists dismantled texts like toys to see how they were put together and how they were used. Whether playfully or seriously, they wrecked havoc with the pomp and circumstance of history and literature, and with the official Grand Narratives done up in capital letters, which stressed certain aspects of the human experience to the detriment and even oblivion of all others. What you don't mention can also be counted as propaganda, or, to use a current word, as spin. Since I came to the United States I found out that my own culture was among those that had been, to a large extent, omitted from the public awareness ever since the First World War. I am therefore sympathetic to, and sometimes even delighted about some of the deeds postmodernism has done for the involuntarily voiceless cultures of others. Quite properly, having a *Room of One's Own* is beneficial for human beings. It is as important as having food to eat and air to breathe. It provides a space where we can use our own mental furniture, our pictures, books, mementos, songs, and flowers. It gives us privacy and psychological freedom. It is the symbolic center of our identity, and that does not mean that it should ever be a narrow, cell-like cavern which affords only myopic views. A home and hospitality belong together. The most cosmopolitan among us, and those who are, in a way, hybrids in knowing two or more societies intimately, are only too well aware of this. They have felt what it means to be strangers. They tend to notice things that are overlooked, and sometimes they see them upside-down.

I found such a thing probably unseen by others in the recent work of David Gress. He was born in Copenhagen of Danish-American parents, studies and works on both continents, lives in Denmark, and seems to have one foot in Europe and the other one in the States. Gress identifies what he calls the concept of the ahistorical (based on ideas, not on actual history) Grand Narrative of the New West, which has dominated American higher education for most of this century. In his intellectual history *From Plato to Nato* (1998), Gress argues that the US adopted the cult of the Greeks from Winkelmann and Goethe, skipped the history of the Old West in spirit if not entirely in letter, jumped directly to the Enlightenment and the founding of the United States, and then developed the Grand Narrative of the New West after World War I at Columbia College in New York and at the "Great Books" program at the University of Chicago. In 1917, the US government asked colleges to prepare "War and Peace" courses. So when the young soldiers returned from **the war to end all wars** they would be sent to college to learn, after the fact, about western civilization, and **why they had fought, and for what**. Scores of teachers were trained to broadcast a vision of the world as constructed in the American Grand Narrative. According to Gress, this well-planned higher education program was designed to turn young men from the farms and the immigrant neighborhoods into good citizens. Great books and great ideas could work, and in only two semesters, against the "barbarization of war" the young had experienced. The teachings, writes Gress, were intended to "turn former soldiers into prospective philosopher kings." Unfortunately the Old West, a symbiosis of Rome, Christianity, and Germanic liberty, as well as much of the actual history, fell through the cracks. To be sure, for a modern nation like the United States there was something embarrassing about the very idea of the Middle Ages, however rich and varied this foundation of actual western civ. was in reality.

So indeed, the Grand Narrative was based on the German 18th century fascination with the ancient Greeks. With these German origins soon forgotten or exorcised, the U.S. story of western civilization had frog-leaped from antiquity all the way to the American Revolution and the Enlightenment with only a few way stations in between. As luck would have it, it was just this particular concept of history that Stanford University students attacked in 1986 with shouts of "Hey, hey, ho, ho, western culture's got to go!" The students felt that the almost sacred Grand Narrative offered idealized, incomplete, and phony interpretations of events. It also left a lot out. The historian Norman Davies wrote that it presented a false view of the European past, a view that was centered on a "WASP West," and on the "Allied scheme of history," which, as Gress puts its, ignored everything that didn't fit into "the simple Plato-to-Nato-scheme of constant improvement."

That was in the late 80's, and today the students are no longer shouting. There has been change, and it would be an exaggeration to say that it is to everyone's liking. Still, today you can go into bookstores and find a selection of Latino (both in English and Spanish), Native American, Chinese, Japanese, Irish, and Black writing, sometimes showcased on special tables and in displays at the front of the store. And in cities where Latino writing isn't offered by the big book store chains, Latino-owned small shops have opened, especially in the Southwest and along the West Coast. But no, you won't find much German writing in translation, and how could you, with only a tiny number of titles from the German-speaking countries being published in English per year. Germany is the quiet and shrinking violet in a rambunctious society and in a potentially big US market. According to the 1990 census, some 23.3 percent of Americans claim to be of German descent, and many of these nearly 60 million people still maintain, or have regained an interest in their background. It is now acceptable to care about such matters. But the interest in things German finds few offerings and slim pickings, although sources on the Internet are growing.

The restraint shown about things German is discreet and estimable, but in a large, active, and diversified country like the United States it is the squeaking wheel that gets the grease. You have to speak up. You have to value your language. And to be represented you have to compete for shelf space and attention like everybody else. It will not be given to you as a reward for good behavior. Once upon a time it was different. Handed to me by the Ohio branch of the family, I own a *Deutsches Erstes Lesebuch Fuer Amerikanische Schulen* von W.H. Weick und C. Grebner, published by American Book Company - New York - Cincinnati - Chicago - in 1886. It was used by seven-year-old children in the second grade, is quite charming, and contains short stories and poetry – including Goethe's "*Ich ging im Walde so für mich hin....*" But if someone decided to do polls about the acquaintance of Americans with German art, science, history, language, letters, or geography today, what would he find? It almost makes me laugh: I bet the results would be dismal. Let's be candid: at the end of this millennium, only a minute number of Americans, and certainly no children in elementary schools, would have ever heard the name Goethe, or Heine, or Heisenberg. People still live in towns named Hamburg, New Bremen, and even Weimar, Texas, but Germany itself has re-acquired the status of *terra incognita* – except perhaps for Bavaria, Beer, and Beethoven. Oh, and add Lederhosen to that. Otherwise the country is now, for all practical purposes, a new white spot on the map - inhabited by strange and imaginary beings.

Although the German white spot is one of the bigger ones, I have found many other white spots on the maps that will (mis)guide us into the 21st century. I ran into them during my years of roaming, when I was visiting various countries in the old fashioned physical manner, preferably off the beaten path. Before long I found white spots in all kinds of places and spaces, most prominently in human minds and perceptions. And eventually it was a shocking, unexpected experience to stumble upon the great unknown in cyberspace. The Internet is already a veritable storehouse of human knowledge. But have no doubt: it is also a jungle out there. A big bad one, red in tooth and claw. Therefore, like the sailors and navigators before them, cybernauts must also face monsters of the deep, landfall adventures, dangers, pitfalls, and the endurance tests of discovery. How can that be? Is there really a new *terra incognita* out there? And why so late, why now, long after all the lands that could be explored have been explored, surveyed, mapped, and photographed by satellites on this shrinking planet of ours? Something must have happened since Gutenberg's printing press enabled us to look around as more or less emancipated individuals. And if so, it must have occurred during the last hundred years, during the calamitous 20th century. That was the time period when governments rationed information, when ideas to shape and manipulate public opinion took hold, and when the mass media came into their own. It is of course impossible to say with any degree of certainty how a modern mythological world came about, but there can be no doubt that it exists, teeming with all the fearful creatures from the old manuscripts, with grotesque beings, fire-spitting dragons, many-headed hydras, one-eyed giants, pale ghosts, and with strange mutants from the urban legends.

At a first level of irony, the *terra incognita* of the early 21st century will be an unintended result of our advanced technological and widely informed age. The one-way communication offered by the mass media during the pre-Internet era facilitated the birth and unchecked multiplication of modern myths which took hold in human minds and blossomed into fantastic forms and shapes. These are constructs of a special kind: once established they are nearly impossible to get rid of. One young German who was brave enough to go out questing as an Internet dragon slayer against historical distortions and outright falsehoods cried out in exasperation: "But it happens again and again....Can you imagine doing this for your whole life?" He will have to. He needs lots of help. He has no idea how many hydras are out there, and how long they last. Still, you can succeed if you persist.

On a second level of irony, increasing numbers of citizens recognized that they had been demoted to being mere watchers. Many didn't like it too well, so they began to reject their role as passive members of an audience. Neil Postman put the essence of the phenomenon into the title of a 1985 book he called *Amusing Ourselves to Death.* Small wonder that being a couch potato lost some of its charm. Mass media consumers grew bored with both entertainment and politics. Rental videos couldn't cure the ennui either. Pop Corn and the circuses lost much of their repetitive attraction. The docile role also clashed fundamentally with the principles and requirements of a democratic society. (In 1996 voting, by those who are eligible, fell to below fifty percent in the US – and of course some persons like it that way).

On a third level of irony, societies are now burdened with the informational offspring their governments and ideological crusaders released into the 20th century in the proclaimed service of national goals. It was done to persuade and motivate their own publics, sell their own political agendas and programs, manufacture consensus, sell and fight wars, invent, dehumanize and demonize enemies, and influence world opinion. Times, governments, and history changed, yet many of the creatures and caricatures of conflict-ridden decades lived on, mutated, and spread in people's minds. Similar to gossip they grew ever more outlandish in the telling. One could also compare the phenomenon to the import of rabbits into Australia: the little darlings lustily engaged in rapid duplication and managed to remain resilient no matter what was done to them.

On a fourth level of irony, governments find it difficult to reign in any of these footloose mythological contraptions which continue to do damage, thereby sabotaging the efforts of diplomacy. Facing up to the chimeras, confronting them, shining a light into their countenances, could deprive them of power. Gradually, they would collapse. Britain's *Economist* points out that many countries have neglected to come to terms with their history. In an article back in April of 1994, it wrote that "nations need to know themselves, and confront their pasts.... For nations as for people, denial of the past can be corrupting....The Germans have achieved a remarkable feat of collective self-analysis and contrition.... Raking over the past is never pleasant, but to forget the lessons of history is worse."

The *Economist* argues that "rigorously frank textbooks at school" would be the place to start in coming closer to the truth", and the "next place for conscience-pricking is an inquisitive press." As things stand, we can't count on such wonderful developments. Instead, we may move even further away from attempts to be truthful.

Considering this situation, it is no wonder that various national histories clash, often ferociously, on the Internet in a search for facts, evidence, and mutually acceptable narratives in open international dialogues and polylogues.

At this point, there are three things that can help us. The first is indeed the Internet, which can function as the new *agora*. The second item are books and publishing, and here I would include economically valid ways of print-on-demand technology (printing one, or a few copies at a time, and making a profit), online publishing, online book selling on an international scale in various languages, and the electronic book itself. The digital versions do not offer the pleasures of touching a real book. But there are compensations: you can dog-ear, text search, annotate, highlight, improve your vocabulary (built-in dictionary), change size of print, curl up with it, and read in the dark from a lighted screen.

Of course no one can predict the future. Who knows, perhaps one day we may reload our libraries like we re-charge batteries or fill tanks in our cars. And down the road, we may honor only exceptional writing of suspected lasting value with fine "real book" editions but publish the bulk of the ephemeral work, for instance each year's crop of bestsellers, as e-books. The book itself will certainly survive just as it did during the shifts from scroll to folio, from hand-copied volume to printing press production, and from hardcover to mass paperback. In the end, it is quality of content, and content itself, that was and will be the most important resource.

The third and last item of help is directly related to the first two, and they all feed into each other. Number three is the surprising surge toward literacy, however changed and contemporary. Juxtaposed to the century's new white spots and its mythological creatures is a strongly revived passion for debate, discourse, discussion, reasoning, and yes, also for satire, parody, laughter, insult, and invective. All this communicative exuberance broke loose as if flood gates had suddenly opened, and it is sweeping a pent-up social silence away like rushing waters. Now there are numerous human voices, making a vast web of international connections across national, linguistic, and cultural borders. To be heard, arguments and thoughts have to be formulated in writing —however short, — and only then can they be clicked off for the jump through cyberspace. In turn, the basic act of writing, and of reasoning and thinking, re-energizes the embattled Gutenberg revolution's shift "from image culture to word culture." Of course the visual will continue to thrive, but we need literacy so citizens will be able to deal with the complexities of public life and make informed decisions. Incidentally, I think US-Americans are an exceedingly verbal people. Listen to them: how agile they are with words! And one can meet little kids who may have fallen behind doing endless tests in school yet love to talk, and sound lively and bright.

The current global chatter marathons rely mostly on the lingua franca of cyberspace – English. Still, as mentioned earlier, using the same language will not prevent us from talking past each other. We live in different environments, and the jolts of code-shifting will be felt frequently. It is part of the challenge, and once it can be at least partly overcome valuable transnational friendships may develop. There is an amazing amount of good writing on the Internet. And at best, it can also be profoundly moving and authentic.

I have now come full circle in revisiting Weimar, the current Cultural City of Europe, in a roundabout way. It is time to reply to the prize question:

Liberating the Future from the Past?
Liberating the Past from the Future?

Can we do it? Perhaps. But we will have to go out into the world and into cyberspace as in a quest, help the dragon slayers, explore our many clashing histories, and tell our own stories – passionately, honestly, and fearlessly. It will take a myriad of small and committed deeds and doings to assemble the foundations, deal with heaps of mental pollution, and fill in the voids. Fittingly, *historein* is a Greek verb, and it means to ask questions.

In his *Fragmente*, Novalis (Friedrich von Hardenberg, 1772-1801) observed that partial history is impossible. To him "every history must be world history, and only in relationship to the whole of history is the historical treatment of a single topic possible." How surprisingly contemporary and interesting it is that this luminous young thinker and poet, living in the provincial surroundings and within the post – Thirty Years' War political patchwork quilt of 18th century Germany, was able to open the curtain for a glimpse into a possible future when such a global perspective of the past could indeed become a requirement without which everything else to come may remain like a house built on sand.